Contents

Words that appear in the glossary are printed in bold, **like this**, the first time they occur in the text.

The Earth's atmosphere

The Earth's atmosphere is the mass of gases that surrounds the planet. These gases are attracted to the surface by the Earth's **gravitational force**. In some places, particles of the atmosphere are found as far as 1600 kilometres (1000 miles) into space. The atmosphere is made up of 78 per cent nitrogen, 21 per cent oxygen and traces of other gases including argon and carbon dioxide. The air in the atmosphere becomes thinner further away from the Earth.

Weathering the troposphere

The atmosphere is divided into layers. We live in the troposphere, which extends 9.6 to 16 kilometres (6 to 10 miles) above the Earth's surface. Air temperature in the troposphere generally decreases with **altitude**. The outermost area of the troposphere is the tropopause, where temperatures average –65 °C (–85 °F). All our weather happens in the troposphere. This layer of gases is also where most of the Earth's air pollution takes place.

Violent rainstorms like hurricanes and typhoons occur naturally in the troposphere, the lowest layer of the atmosphere.

Into the stratosphere

Beyond the troposphere, at altitudes of 9.6 to 50 kilometres (6 to 31 miles), lies the stratosphere. **Ozone** (O_3) in the stratosphere protects our skin and eyes from harmful **ultraviolet** (UV) rays in sunlight. But down in the troposphere, ozone is a major component of smog.

UV light is absorbed by ozone in the upper portions of the stratosphere, heating the outermost layers to temperatures as high as –2 °C (28 °F). Temperatures in the layers closer to the tropopause are generally much lower, at around –55 °C (–67 °F).

The final frontiers

The mesosphere, which means middle sphere, extends from 48 to 80 kilometres (30 to 50 miles) above the surface of the Earth. The mesosphere is the coldest part of the Earth's atmosphere. Temperatures drop to –100 °C (–148 °F) and are cold enough to freeze water vapour into ice clouds! You can sometimes see these clouds, known as noctilucent clouds, after sunset.

Above the mesosphere lies the thermosphere. Its lower boundary begins 85 kilometres (53 miles) above the Earth. The name thermosphere means heat sphere. During the day, temperatures in the thermosphere can reach a high of 1475 °C (2687 °F). Nighttime temperatures dip to 225 °C (437 °F). The upper boundary of the thermosphere lies 600 kilometres (373 miles) above sea level. Beyond that is space.

Noctilucent clouds over Finland. These are normally seen in the middle of the night in summer and at high latitudes.

The equatorial bulge

The Earth's atmosphere is thickest at the equator and thinnest at the poles. As the Earth rotates on its axis the force of the movement pulls some of the atmospheric gases from the poles towards the equator, causing the atmosphere to bulge around the equator.

What is air pollution?

Air pollution occurs whenever **waste** products mix with the air. Most of the waste products causing air pollution come from burning fuel to power vehicles and heat buildings. Industries and rubbish burning also release **pollutants**. This is a frightening thought as the average adult breathes about 13,200 litres (3000 gallons) of air each day. In many areas, such as Los Angeles and Mexico City, the air is so filled with pollutants it threatens people's health. In the USA, more than 46 million people live in areas with dangerously polluted air.

An old problem

People have been burning wood and **fossil fuels** since prehistoric times. Our human ancestors burned fuels to keep warm. Romans burned coal to light their lamps in AD 100. Historical documents describe Seneca, tutor of the Roman emperor Nero, who complained about the smoke from wood fires. In the Middle Ages (the period from AD 500 to AD 1500) large cities began to use coal more than wood. Burning coal produces even sootier smoke than wood fires.

The Industrial Revolution

From the 1700s to the 1800s, during the **Industrial Revolution**, air pollution levels skyrocketed. Starting with the UK, European countries began to develop large-scale factory production in place of home-based industries. Large quantities of coal were burned to provide steam power to run these factories.

Flame from a chemical plant escaping into the atmosphere. The Industrial Revolution paved the way for even more air pollution.

World population explosion!

In the last hundred years, world population has **quadrupled**. Most of the growth occurred in the 50 years after World War II. At the start of the 1900s, global population was an estimated 1.6 billion. This grew to 6 billion by the year 2000.

As the human population continues to increase at a rapid rate, the number of vehicles, homes and industries also increases. These are new sources of pollution. As a result, air pollution becomes a bigger problem with time.

Air pollution is most dangerous in and around cities. But it is present to some extent everywhere.

Motor vehicles

Motor vehicles were invented in the late 19th century. By 1994, there were 642 million motor vehicles in the world. One out of every ten people owned a car. By 1999, the number of motor vehicles had increased to 780 million. Vehicles release increasing amounts of pollutants into the environment. In Japan, 90 per cent of air pollution comes from the **exhaust** gases of vehicles.

Industrial Revolution timeline

1709
coke, a form of coal, replaces charcoal and wood as fuel

1719
the first British textile factory is built

1773
cotton cloth is produced in factories; before 1773, weavers made cotton cloth at home

1800
the battery is invented

1712
the steam engine is invented

1733
the first flying shuttle is built, allowing materials to be woven wider and faster

1784
homes are lit by lamps powered by coal gas

1813
the number of people employed in factories exceeds that in farms

1867
the number of industries quadruple; first mention of industrial smog in London

1802
the first steam boat is built in Scotland

1831
the electric generator is invented

1885
the first motor vehicle is manufactured

1903
the first aeroplane flies successfully

Forms of air pollution

Airborne pollutants react with one another in the air, producing new forms of pollution like smog and **acid rain**. These chemical reactions speed up in warm, sunny weather. Their products can travel long distances and become more harmful the further they get from the source.

Smog

Smog is a combination of smoke and fog. The sources of pollutants in smog include fire smoke, paints and the exhaust fumes of vehicles. During the summer, sunlight reacts with smog giving it a brown tinge. In some major cities, such as New York and London, the smog has a greyish colour – the result of higher concentrations of ash, soot and other **particulates**.

Smog clouds the view of the River Thames in London. In 1952, 'killer' smog took the lives of some 4000 people in London.

Acid rain has destroyed vegetation in some areas of the Blue Mountains in New South Wales, Australia.

Acid rain

Acid rain is a broad term used to describe rainfall that has a pH of less than five. The level of pH (potential of hydrogen) of a substance determines if it is **acidic** or not. Rain becomes acidic when pollutants in the air **dissolve** in rain water. Even in unpolluted areas, rainfall is slightly acidic. The pH of rainfall in the countryside is around six. Rain becomes more acidic in towns and cities. The pH of rainfall in most urban areas is around four.

The features on this statue have been eroded by chemicals in acid rain.

What is acid rain made of?

Airborne pollutants react in the atmosphere with water and oxygen to form acidic compounds like sulphuric acid (H_2SO_4) and nitric acid (HNO_3). Sulphuric acid is an odourless, colourless and oily liquid. Nitric acid is a colourless liquid. In moist air, it releases fumes strong enough to choke you. Both sulphuric acid and nitric acid are very **corrosive**. These acidic compounds return to the land dissolved in precipitation. This is water that falls to the Earth as acid rain, snow, hail, fog or mist.

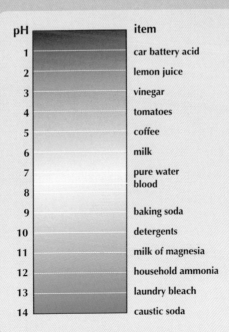

pH	item
1	car battery acid
2	lemon juice
3	vinegar
4	tomatoes
5	coffee
6	milk
7	pure water / blood
8	
9	baking soda
10	detergents
11	milk of magnesia
12	household ammonia
13	laundry bleach
14	caustic soda

Quick facts about the pH scale

We measure the pH value of substances using the pH scale. The pH scale ranges from zero to fourteen. **Neutral** substances have a pH of seven. Acidic substances have a pH level lower than seven. **Alkaline** substances have a pH level higher than seven. The scale to the left shows the pH value of some everyday things.

Measuring air pollution

Scientists and health authorities measure air pollution to find out if the environment is safe to live in. Modern techniques for measuring air pollution take one of two forms. They either measure **emissions** from a source or the type and number of pollutant particles in the atmosphere.

Ringelmann's smoke chart

Ringelmann's smoke chart has been used since 1932, making it the oldest method of measuring air pollution. The chart has a scale of one to five, corresponding to a colour scale from light grey to black. Scientists observe smoke rising from a source approximately 16 metres away and compare the smoke colour to the chart. Dense and heavy smoke corresponds to a darker grey, while the lighter shades indicate that the smoke is not so dense. In the USA, smoke is considered dense if it has the same colour as a grade three shade.

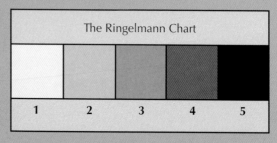

The Ringelmann Chart

1   2   3   4   5

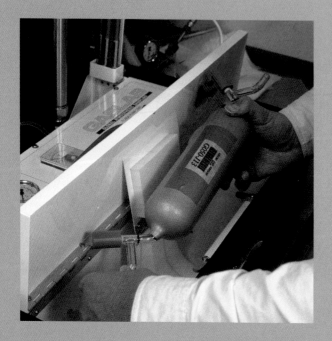

Measurements from a source

Health authorities sometimes measure the concentration of pollutants from sources like factory chimneys. These measurements are known as emission measurements. They are taken to ensure that industrial plants and vehicles are not releasing too much pollution into the air. Environmental officers collect samples of the gas in containers shaped like test-tubes. They calculate the percentage of pollutants in the sample and the amount of exhaust gas released per second. This helps them estimate how much pollution is released in a certain period of time.

Gas cylinder being filled with a sample of air. Technicians look for gases that trap heat in the atmosphere and those that destroy ozone.

Health and environmental authorities check air quality by examining the content of atmospheric air. This is known as atmospheric measurement. They conduct atmospheric measurement using gas chromatography. Chromatography is a method used to separate mixtures into their various **components**. It allows the authorities to identify the components and measure their quantities.

A sample of polluted air is injected into a non-reactive gas like helium. The gas mixture travels along a tube containing reactive chemicals. These chemicals react with the components in the sample. Components that are most reactive move slowly through the tube. Components that are less reactive move faster. The air mixture is separated into its components as they travel at different speeds.

The MAPS instrument has travelled aboard the Space Shuttle four times. The first mission was in November 1981.

New developments

Scientists have developed instruments that detect tiny pollutant particles. Some of these particles are 25,000 times smaller than the diameter of a human hair! NASA established its Measurement of Air Pollution from Satellites (MAPS) program in 1981. Satellite-mounted sensors measure carbon monoxide levels around the Earth. The program also monitors how widely pollutants are distributed.

Major gas pollutants

Many different processes combine to cause air pollution. These processes and the chemicals involved in them have unique characteristics. The most common pollutants include sulphur dioxide, carbon compounds and nitrogen oxides.

Sulphur dioxide

Sulphur dioxide (SO_2) is a colourless substance with a strong, **pungent** odour. At temperatures colder than –10 °C (14 °F) sulphur dioxide turns into a liquid. It exists as a gas at higher temperatures. Sulphur dioxide is a useful chemical. It is used in the manufacture of sulphuric acid and for bleaching paper in the paper industry. Some chefs dip food items like french fries and peach slices in a weak sulphur dioxide solution to stop them from turning brown. But in large quantities sulphur dioxide is also a harmful chemical. It is one of the main components of acid rain.

Paper manufacturers combine sulphur dioxide with water to form sulphurous acid which serves as a bleach. When accidentally released, the acid pollutes lakes, rivers and streams and harms any wildlife and plants that grow there.

Forest fires not only release pollutants such as carbon dioxide into the air, they destroy the natural habitats of birds and animals that live in the forest.

Carbon compounds

Carbon monoxide (CO) is an invisible, odourless and poisonous gas. Too much carbon monoxide in the environment can kill you. When we breathe in carbon monoxide, it replaces oxygen in our bloodstream. As a result our cells suffocate from lack of oxygen. People exposed to high levels of carbon monoxide over long periods of time suffer from brain damage.

Volatile organic compounds (VOCs) and carbon dioxide are two other types of carbon-rich gas found in polluted air. VOCs contain carbon and substances that **vaporize** easily. Some paints and cleaning fluids are made with VOCs. Carbon dioxide is a gas that is produced during burning, when living things **respire** and when animal or vegetable matter decays.

Exhaust fumes from motor vehicles are responsible for almost half of the VOCs and nitrogen dioxide, and nearly 90 per cent of the carbon monoxide found in urban air.

Nitrogen oxides

A pair of nitrogen compounds – nitric oxide (NO) and nitrogen dioxide (NO_2) – make up nitrogen oxides. The human eye cannot detect nitric oxide. Our bodies use nitric oxide to transport oxygen and send nerve signals. On its own, nitric oxide is not harmful to the environment. But it combines with atmospheric gases and exhaust fumes to form nitrogen dioxide, a more harmful compound. This foul-smelling brown gas plays an important role in the creation of smog. It is a major component of acid rain and reacts with other chemicals to create nitric acid.

The oxide cycle

A strange cycle involving nitrogen oxides, oxygen and ozone happens in the atmosphere. In sunlight, nitrogen dioxide molecules break down into one **atom** of oxygen and nitric oxide. The atom of oxygen combines with two other oxygen atoms in the air, forming ozone. Then, the nitric oxide reacts with the oxygen atoms in ozone, producing nitrogen dioxide, and the cycle begins again.

If VOCs are present, they combine with nitric oxide to form nitrogen dioxide. When this happens, there is less nitric oxide in the air to combine with ozone and continue the cycle. The ozone builds up and smog forms.

Particulate matter in polluted air

Air pollutants fall into two broad categories: some are gases and some are particulate matter. Particulate matter is tiny specks of material found in the air. They are present in smoke, dust and soot. Individual particles of these pollutants may be too small to see with the naked eye. In high concentrations, they appear as clouds of soot, dust or grey haze.

Soot

The fine, black material floating from a bonfire is soot. Soot particles are usually less than 1 millimetre in diameter. Soot is mainly made up of carbon and is also known as carbon black. Carbon black is a common raw material in many industrial products including vehicle tyres, paint and printer and copier ink. Factories produce carbon black for industry by burning carbon-rich fuels like petroleum.

Making charcoal by burning wood at high temperature. Soot from burning wood can irritate the eyes, nose and throat. Soot also discolours buildings, clothes and furniture.

Pollen dust

In Latin, the word pollen means dust or fine flour. Pollen grains are tiny particles produced by male flower parts. The production of pollen is often seasonal. Flowers release pollen in different quantities depending on weather conditions and the time of day. The North American ragweed, for example, produces most pollen in the mornings of early September. Many plant species release their pollen grains when the weather is dry, warm and windy.

The vibrant yellow of the ragweed flower disguises a hidden danger. Its pollen prompts hay fever for many people in North America. Note the spines of the pollen grain in this magnified image. The spines allow the grain to attach to insects, which then carry the pollen to other plants.

Mould

Nature also produces **mould** particulates all year round. Mould thrives in warm weather, but it can grow in both dry and wet conditions. Mould releases **spores** into the air. Mould spores are too tiny to be seen, but you can see mould growing in black, green or grey patches.

Eating dust

Around 80 per cent of the fine, dry material we call dust is really dander. Dander is the flakes of dead skin that fall off humans and animals. We each shed around 5.7 grams of dander per week. Dust mites are tiny animals that feed on dust and dander. They belong to the spider family. Eighty per cent of the dust mite body is made up of water. Not surprisingly, dust mites like to live in **humid** environments. They cannot survive dry, hot weather because their transparent bodies offer little protection from sunlight. The picture on the right is a scanning electron micrograph (SEM) of a dust mite.

Human causes of pollution

Most of the Earth's air pollution starts with human activity. Humans pollute both the outdoor and indoor environments. Most of us are aware that outdoor air pollution is harmful to our health. But indoor air pollution can be even more dangerous. The level of pollutants is often two to five times higher indoors, and in some cases as much as 100 times higher than outdoor levels. People living in developed countries like the USA spend 90 per cent of their time indoors. This means that the average American is breathing in highly polluted air for most of his or her life.

Fuel combustion

The main components of fuel are carbon and hydrogen. When fuels combust, or burn, they combine with oxygen in the air to form new chemical compounds. These include substances that contaminate the air. Sometimes there is not enough oxygen available for the complete combustion of carbon-rich fuels. When that happens, soot, nitrogen oxides, carbon dioxide and carbon monoxide form.

Cooling towers of a power station in Staffordshire, England. Note the houses near the foot of the towers. Humans are both the cause of the pollution and the victims of the pollution.

Indoor and outdoor pollution

A major cause of indoor pollution is burning fuel to heat offices, houses and other buildings. Air pollution also happens when people cook on faulty stoves that do not burn fuel completely. These stoves release a lot of soot particles into the air. Many cleaning products release volatile organic compounds (VOCs) into the air. Others give off poisonous gases such as ammonia, which combine with acidic gases like nitric acid to form dust-sized particles. These airborne specks cause problems in the lungs when inhaled. Laundry bleaches contain chlorine, a strong-smelling gas.

Outdoors, electric power plants that burn coal or oil release pollutants into the atmosphere. These pollutants include nitrogen oxides, sulphur dioxide, particulates and carbon dioxide. Fuel combustion also powers vehicle engines. In the USA, motor vehicles are responsible for nearly 90 per cent of the carbon monoxide in city air.

Smoke from wood-burning stoves contains higher levels of hazardous air pollutants than smoke flowing from oil- or gas-burning stoves.

Secondhand cigarette smoke

Every day, millions of people are exposed to cigarette smoke at home, in restaurants and in other public areas. Scientists believe that of the 4000 chemicals in tobacco smoke, 43 may cause cancer. One of these chemicals is tar, which damages the tiny cilia hairs in our airways. These hairs help to filter out harmful chemicals in our atmosphere. When they are destroyed, we are no longer protected from harmful substances in the air we breathe.

The Edmonton Incinerator burns refuse from London boroughs to generate electricity.

Disposing of solid waste

One of the ways local authorities get rid of household and industrial waste is by burning. Burning waste produces thick, black smoke and pollutants such as hydrocarbons, acidic gases, nitrogen dioxide, sulphur dioxide and carbon. Batteries, fluorescent light bulbs and magazine dyes burn to produce **heavy metals**, which escape into the environment as incinerator ashes.

Natural sources of pollution

Not all pollution is connected to human activity. For example, plants, grass and trees are a source of pollen. And approximately 10 per cent of polluting ozone in the troposphere is transported from the stratosphere. In some cases, natural sources of air pollution have a greater impact on the environment than human activity. Volcanoes, **decomposition** and forest fires release approximately 1.2 times more sulphuric pollutants each year than industries and vehicles.

Volcanoes

Molten rock, or magma, contains gaseous pollutants like nitrogen oxides, which dissolve under high pressure. When magma flows to the surface, the pressure on it decreases because there is less weight above it. The dissolved gases escape into the environment as deadly fumes. Volcanic eruptions release high levels of sulphur dioxide and particulates into the air.

   Large-scale volcanic eruptions can choke the atmosphere with particulates, blocking sunlight from reaching the surface. When that happens, the Earth's weather becomes colder. Green plants, which need sunlight to **photosynthesize**, start to die.

The volcanic dust and ash that are released during an eruption are minute airborne particles. They can scorch vegetation and kill people by suffocation.

Lightning is a great electrical spark that occurs in the sky. Lightning strikes the Earth about 100 times each second.

Other natural sources

Every day, approximately 51,000 tonnes of nitrogen oxides are released from the oceans, the decomposition of decaying matter and lightning strikes. Tiny marine organisms decompose animal matter such as excretion, releasing nitrogen oxides in the process.

Lightning bolts heat air up to 30,000 °C (54,000 °F). The heat breaks down nitrogen and oxygen gases in the atmosphere into their individual atoms. After lightning strikes, the air cools down. The atoms of oxygen and hydrogen recombine to form polluting nitrogen oxides.

Radon

Radon is a colourless, odourless and tasteless gas produced by the **radioactive decay** of radium, a metallic element. Radium occurs naturally in rocks and soil and decomposes over time. Radon can be found in granite rock, bricks and concrete. Rock and soil in Devon and Cornwall in south-west England have the highest amount of radon in the UK. Some parts of your home, like the basement, may also have higher levels of radon because they are close to soil. Radon enters buildings through cracks in walls and floors. In the UK, one out of every twenty people suffering from lung cancer has lived in a radon-polluted environment.

Green sun, blue moon

Did you know that the term 'once in a blue moon' probably came from the eruption on Krakatoa, a volcanic island in Indonesia? In 1883, Krakatoa erupted with such force that volcanic material was thrown 48 kilometres (30 miles) high and fell over 800,000 square kilometres (300,000 square miles). Volcanic dust remained in the atmosphere for over two years. Through the dust, the setting sun looked green and the moon appeared to be blue.

Air pollution and ecosystems

An ecosystem is a web formed by the interactions among plants, animals and their environment. The environment includes the soil, air, water sources and climate of an area. Living things are connected to their environment. Plants, animals and humans depend on each other for food. Living things also need the right environment to grow in. Destroying one part of an ecosystem will damage the other parts of the ecosystem as well.

Soil nutrients and trees

As rainfall **percolates** through soils, it drains nutrients away from plant roots. This process is known as leaching. The rate of leaching increases when rain is acidic. Acid rain contains hydrogen, which reacts with the minerals in the soil. When this happens, nutrients such as calcium, potassium and magnesium dissolve in the rain water and are washed downwards. Trees need these nutrients to grow or they start to die.

This pine tree in the Blue Mountains of Australia is stunted from lack of nutrients.

Plants and pests

Scientists discovered that plants surrounded by badly polluted air are not able to grow properly. These plants photosynthesize and build up plant tissue more slowly than plants in clean air. When they are attacked by pests, such as the bean beetle, these plants repair their damaged parts slowly. The damaged parts are vulnerable to further attack.

Bean beetles and their larvae feed on the underside of bean leaves. They chew on the softer parts of the leaf, leaving the tougher leaf tissues behind. The attacked leaf has a lacy appearance and dies in two days. In Mexico, large areas of bean farms have been destroyed by bean beetles. Besides the bean plant, bean beetles also attack plants like cowpea, clover and alfalfa.

Gone with the wind

Pollutants travel with the wind. High levels of ozone and sulphur dioxide from industrial areas can affect the countryside. Acid rain from the industries in one country affects neighbouring countries. For example, winds travelling from the south-west to the north-east carry pollutants and acid rain from the industries in the mid-western USA and central Canada. The winds deposit the pollutants in the rural areas of the north-eastern USA and south-eastern Canada.

Larvae of the Mexican bean beetle. This beetle species is one of the most destructive insect pests. They cause the most damage in July and August.

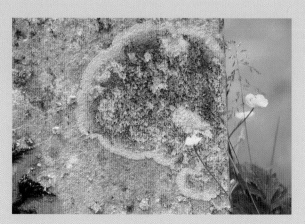

Lichens alert!

In the 1800s, scientists discovered that air pollution was killing **lichens** in European cities like Paris. Lichens do not have a protective covering on their leaves. When lichens absorb acid rain, sulphur dioxide breaks down the **chlorophyll** in the leaves. They are not able to photosynthesize and they die. This means scientists can use lichens to study air pollution. In the USA, a lichen community **indicator** studies lichens growing on rotting wood, trees and shrubs to work out the impact of air pollution on the trees.

Drought in Africa

Africa is the second largest continent in the world. It lies between the Atlantic and Indian Oceans, to the south of the European continent. Warm, moist winds from the southern **hemisphere** form rain clouds over northern Africa. The Sahel, the dry region south of the Sahara Desert, receives as little as 200 millimetres of rain per year. Scientists studying rainfall in the tropical regions found that air pollution disrupts rainfall in northern Africa. The sources of this pollution are industries in African cities, North America, Europe and Asia.

The Sahel region in Africa has been especially dry since 1968. Crops fail because there is no rain. Not only that, locusts have been known to destroy whatever crops might have successfully grown.

Too small to fall

Using satellite images, scientists discovered that clouds that form in dirty air produce half the rainfall of clouds that form in clean air. For rain to fall, water vapour in the air must condense around **nuclei** to form water droplets. Rain falls when the water droplets gather together and become too heavy to stay in the air. Sulphur dioxide particulates in smog can be as small as 0.001 millimetres in diameter. These sulphur particulates remain airborne for up to twenty days and act as nuclei for clouds. But the sulphur dioxide nuclei are so small that the water droplets do not combine to form raindrops.

Dirty clouds, no rain

Most of the rain in northern Africa falls in the Intertropical Convergence Zone (ITCZ). This is a belt of thunderstorms parallel to the equator. The ITCZ is the zone in which warm, moist wind flowing from the southern hemisphere meets the dry, cool wind from the northern hemisphere.

The tiny nuclei in polluted air reflect light. Compared to clean-air clouds, clouds in polluted air reflect more of the Sun's light back to space. As a result of dirty clouds in the northern hemisphere, oceans in the northern hemisphere receive less of the Sun's energy. They are cooler than oceans in the southern hemisphere. The cool, dry northerly winds strengthen and push the ITCZ southwards, away from the Sahel. Rainfall in northern Africa decreases.

Ethiopian women fighting over water after a severe drought. Drought often leads to famine and diseases such as malaria, cholera and dengue fever.

Belt of thunder

The position of the ITCZ changes throughout the year. In February, the ITCZ lies between 7 degrees north of the equator to 18 degrees south of the equator. In August, it lies around 3 degrees north of the equator, over India and Southeast Asia.

Drought after drought

People in the Sahel face the threat of **drought** every year. The region has had eight droughts since the 1860s. From 1968 to 1973, a prolonged drought killed hundreds of thousands of people. In Ethiopia alone, 200,000 people died. Rainfall fell to 60 per cent of its normal level. Plants and livestock died of thirst and the food supply ran low. Some people had to eat tree bark, which did not have the proteins and minerals they needed to live. Many died from **malnutrition**.

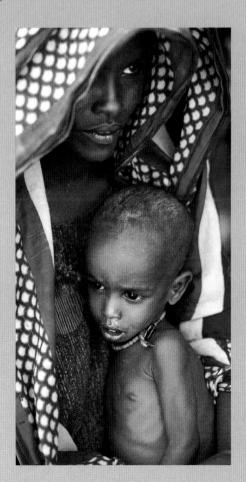

Air pollution and plants

Sulphur dioxide, chlorine and ozone in polluted air are harmful to plants. Plants growing in heavily polluted areas often have yellowish leaves and black or brown leaf tips. These plants may never bear flowers or fruit.

Starving trees

Chlorophyll is a green pigment needed by plants for photosynthesis. Air pollution destroys chlorophyll in leaves, turning them brownish-yellow or black. Sulphur dioxide in acid rain also clogs up the **stomata** of leaves, preventing them from photosynthesizing properly. When this happens, the trees cannot make enough food to grow. Their trunks cannot grow strong and they start to bend. As a result, trees do not reach their maximum height. Some trees also start to shed their leaves.

These witch hazel leaves have been damaged by ozone. While ozone in the upper atmosphere protects the Earth, ozone in the lower atmosphere contributes to air pollution, which affects plants and other living things.

Root rot

Acid rain prevents roots from developing properly. The root networks of affected trees do not spread as far as those of healthy trees. The roots of trees help anchor them to the soil. Trees affected by acid rain are less stable in strong winds and may fall easily.

Rain formed in polluted air contains metallic substances like aluminium, lead, zinc, copper and chromium. These chemicals damage tree roots, leaving the roots vulnerable to attack by **bacteria** and fungi.

Stripped of protection

Many plants and trees, including pine, spruce and fir, have a waxy coating on their leaves. This coating protects the leaves from harmful chemicals in the environment and prevents too much precipitation from collecting on the leaves. Air pollution corrodes this protective leaf wax. As the damaged leaves absorb sulphur dioxide in acid rain, a chemical reaction happens. The leaves start to lose natural organic minerals like calcium and magnesium. Plants lacking calcium develop leaves with curved tips. Magnesium is needed to make the green pigment chlorophyll. The leaves of plants without enough magnesium start to turn yellow and the plant may die.

Frost bite

Plants that grow in temperate regions often have thick **cuticles** and bark. The cuticles and bark are like a coat around the plant. They trap heat in the plant and prevent water in the plant from freezing. Acid rain damages the cuticles and bark and the trees are no longer protected from the cold. **Frost injury** kills flowers and young leaves.

Death in the Black Triangle

The Black Triangle is an area straddling Dresden (Germany), Wroclaw (Poland) and Prague (Czech Republic). There are eight mountain ranges in the area, including the Ore Mountains and the Giant Mountains along the Czech-Polish border. The tallest mountains are the Karkonosze Mountains, which peak at 1602 metres above sea level. Lignite, a soft brown coal, is mined in the mountain regions of the Black Triangle. The Black Forest (Germany) and other forests of fir, pine and spruce grow on the mountains.

Power plants

The Black Triangle is the industrial centre of Europe. The main industries are lignite power plants. Lignite has a high sulphur content. Burning lignite releases high levels of sulphur dioxide and particulates. The air in the Black Triangle has one of the highest levels of sulphur worldwide but efforts are being made to control the pollution. Other pollutants released include acidic gases and metals like aluminium and lead.

A lignite strip mine near Cologne, Germany. In strip mining, soil and rock are first removed from the surface to reach the coal deposits that lie beneath. There is no tunnelling in this method of mining.

Black and balding trees

Scientists found that after the 1960s, trees in the Black Triangle died younger and grew at a slower rate than elsewhere. Acid rain corrodes the wax coating and chlorophyll of the leaves, turning them brownish-yellow or black. As a result, the trees cannot make enough food to grow. Some of the trees shed so many of their leaves they look like dead trees. The shedding starts from the upper part of the tree, called the crown, before it spreads to the rest of the tree.

Up to 1000 square kilometres (386 square miles) of forest in the Black Triangle have died from air pollution. Early in the 1960s, conifers in the Black Forest started dying and then the problem spread to the oak and beech trees. Scientists named this phenomenon *Waldsterben*, which means forest decline.

Bathing in poison

Dirty air covers the forest every day. For about 180 days per year, the pH level of the air falls to four. The air contaminates the soils and the pollutants damage seedlings.

These seedlings can only grow if they get enough nutrients from the soil.

Balding trees in the Czech Republic. The leaves have been destroyed by acid rain.

First growth

The earliest effect of acid rain may be a sudden growth spurt. The trees grow taller and bigger and sprout flowers and leaves faster. Why does this happen? Plants need nitrogen to make protein and to grow. Although nitrogen is abundant in the atmosphere, plants can only use dissolved nitrogen. Nitrogen oxides dissolve in acid rain and seep into the soil. The roots of the trees soak up the nitrogen and transport it to the other parts of the tree.

Air pollution and animals

Animals living in polluted areas suffer from air pollution in three main ways. They breathe in polluted air, consume particulate matter or absorb harmful gases through their skins. The pollutants that cause the most damage to animals include sulphur dioxide, nitrogen oxides, volatile organic compounds (VOCs), heavy metals and ozone.

Flying in dirty air

Air pollution is harmful to birds that fly with their mouths open to catch insects. They swallow polluted air and consume insects poisoned by pollution. Affected birds include the pied flycatcher. Studies have shown that pied flycatchers living around metal-processing plants in Finland lay eggs with thinner shells than normal. Many nestlings develop spindly, weak leg bones.

A Greater Roadrunner having its meal.

Under the skin

Earthworms and **amphibians** have moist, soft skin that absorbs oxygen from the atmosphere. Blood vessels carry the oxygen from the skin to other parts of the body. These animals also absorb air pollution through their skin and store heavy metals like copper, zinc and lead in their bodies. Animals like birds and snakes prey on earthworms and amphibians, consuming the poison at the same time.

Apart from acid rain, water can also be polluted when toxic wastes from industries seep into lakes or rivers. The pollution upsets the natural balance of life in the water. Other sources of water pollution include fertilizers, sewage and livestock wastes.

Acid water

The dissolved pollutants in acid rain acidify lakes and ponds. When the pH level of lake or pond water reaches six, prawns, crabs and other **crustaceans** start to die. The shells of these animals dissolve in acidic environments. Fish like salmon and trout cannot live in acidic waters and they die. Mosses begin to grow along the shores of the lake or pond.

As water becomes more acidic and the pH level of the lake reaches five, the number of insects, including black flies and their larvae, starts to increase. As the acidity of the water increases, the fish population decreases and may be totally wiped out.

Gene mutations

Scientists think that air pollution may cause the genes of animals to **mutate**. Scientists discovered that seagulls found near steel mills in Canada have abnormal genes. Tests showed that these seagulls have genes that may cause them to develop cancer in the future. Their offspring develop abnormally too. University students in Canada also discovered abnormal genes in mice exposed to polluted air from a steel mill.

Pig farms in North Carolina

North Carolina is a beautiful, rural state in the south-eastern USA. Since 1990, the number of pigs in the eastern part of the state has quadrupled. There are approximately 10 million pigs in that part of the state. The stench from pig farms and pig waste is a major source of air pollution in North Carolina. Pig waste also seeps into the ground, contaminating the water supply.

Pig waste

The North Carolina pigs produce more than 17.2 million tonnes of waste each year. Every day, they produce 47,170 tonnes of waste, or 11,000 times more waste than the average Western family. As animal waste decomposes, a colourless and pungent gas called ammonia is released. Pig farms produce more ammonia than the decomposition of household and factory waste in North Carolina combined. Studies have shown that the pigs in North Carolina release more than 76 million kilograms of ammonia per year. This is 73 per cent of the ammonia produced by farms in North Carolina each year.

Effects of ammonia poisoning

As a result of ammonia poisoning, the pigs suffer from illnesses of the stomach and respiratory system. People who live up to 3.2 kilometres (2 miles) away from the pig farms are at higher risk of developing bronchitis and asthma. The strong stench not only makes their living environment unpleasant, it causes headaches and nausea.

Asthma is a respiratory condition in which the airways in the lungs become narrower. Sufferers cannot breathe easily. This girl is inhaling special medication that will help her breathe.

Raining ammonia

Ammonia in the atmosphere dissolves in rain. Ammonia in rainfall enters lakes and rivers in North Carolina. Ammonia is a fertilizer and it causes algae blooms in lakes. Algae blooms happen when a lake suddenly becomes nutrient-rich. Algae feed on the nutrients and grow rapidly. Algae and other plants release carbon dioxide at night and when they decompose. As the lake becomes choked with algae, they absorb more and more oxygen. As a result, other plants and fish are deprived of oxygen and die.

Algae blooms in this lake have killed the fish. Algae are simple organisms that live in water. Some species of algae multiply rapidly in water that is polluted by sewage and fertilizers.

Getting rid of waste

Pig farmers flush pig waste into open pits up to 32,370 square metres large. The solid waste sinks to the bottom of the pits where it decomposes. The farmers collect the liquid from the top of the pits and spray it on abandoned fields. The waste seeps through the soil and pollutes groundwater sources. More than one-third of the groundwater in North Carolina is contaminated by pig waste.

Air pollution and people

People spending a few hours in polluted air may develop irritations of their respiratory systems. These symptoms disappear when the people leave the polluted environment. But people who live in permanently polluted air may develop illnesses that can kill them.

Health

In heavily polluted areas, people suffer from coughs and tightness in the chest. They may also feel a burning sensation in their eyes. Scientists and doctors think that people who spend years breathing polluted air have a higher risk of developing bronchitis and heart disease. Nitrogen oxides in smog damage lung tissue. Scientists estimate that up to 50,000 people in the USA have died from air pollution-related illnesses. In the UK, health authorities estimate that up to 10,000 people die from the effects of pollutant particulates per year.

Acid rain

Acid rain corrodes buildings, statues and bridges. Building materials like marble, sandstone and limestone contain calcium. Calcium reacts with sulphuric acid to form gypsum. Gypsum crumbles easily and the building or statue breaks down. In 1967, the bridge over the Ohio River in the USA collapsed after years of acid rain attack. This accident killed 46 people.

The paintwork on this building has been damaged by acid rain.

*Heavy traffic on a major highway in
Chile. Note the smog in the background.*

Smog gets in your eyes

In some major cities, smog is so thick
people cannot see clearly. When
volatile organic compounds (VOCs),
nitrogen oxides and dust react in
sunlight, they form photochemical
smog. Photochemical smog is a
phenomenon caused by the action of
sunlight on the exhaust gases from
motor vehicles and factories.

In 1948, twenty people died from
the effects of photochemical fog in
Pennsylvania, USA. Photochemical
smog also hangs over Los Angeles.
Aircraft pilots in Los Angeles cannot see
clearly beyond 4.8 kilometres (3 miles)
in the fog, making landing dangerous.
Smogs were common in London until
the British Parliament passed the Clean
Air Act in 1956. The last major smog in
London happened in December 1962.
That caused 106 deaths.

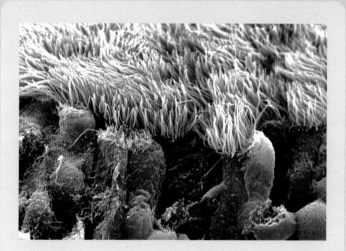

The nose filter

Our noses filter the air we inhale. The human nose traps 99
per cent of pollutant particulates larger than 10 microns. The
rest enter the windpipe and the lungs. Particulates with a
diameter smaller than 4 microns, like pollen grains, can trigger
asthma and hay fever attacks. The photograph shows a section
of the lining of the nasal cavity. The cylindrical cells are
topped with microscopic hair-like structures called cilia. The
cilia are covered with a sticky mucus that traps dust and other
inhaled particles.

Indonesia's blaze haze

Indonesia is located in Southeast Asia, below Peninsular Malaysia, and consists of more than 13,600 islands. The total land area of Indonesia is around 2 million square kilometres (772,200 square miles). Ten per cent of the world's rainforest grows in Indonesia. Indonesia has two seasons. The rainy season lasts from December to March, and the dry season occurs between May and September each year.

An Indonesian farmer in Borneo sets fire to grassland to prepare for the planting season. Worsening haze from fires affects not only the people's health but also the country's economy.

Slash-and-burn

Farmers in Indonesia use the slash-and-burn method to clear forests. Farmers chop down trees and cut the undergrowth before burning all the vegetation. The fire clears the land and the ashes contain minerals that seep into the soil. This increases the fertility of the soil. Crops such as rubber and oil palm are planted in the clearing. After about three years, the plot is left to fallow, or rest, for up to twenty years. After that, the farmers clear the forest again. In 1998, farmers burned up to 24,282 square kilometres (9375 square miles) of Indonesian forest for agriculture.

School children in Borneo wear masks to protect themselves from the choking haze.

Beyond borders

In 1997, the dry season lasted longer than usual. There was no rain to stop the slash-and-burn fires that farmers set and they burned out of control. The fires destroyed more than 99,982 square kilometres (38,603 square miles) of forest and plantation land. The haze spread to the neighbouring countries of Singapore and Malaysia. The thick blanket of smoke drastically reduced visibility in the Malacca Strait between Sumatra (Indonesia) and Peninsular Malaysia. Crew onboard ships could not see clearly in the smog, making navigation difficult. In 1999, the low visibility resulted in the collision of a tanker and a barge in the Malacca Strait, killing twelve people.

Effects on health

In 1997, the level of particulates in the air in Sarawak (Malaysia) was twenty times higher than normal. The haze triggered asthma attacks, severe coughing, breathing difficulties and eye and skin irritations. In the Klang Valley (Malaysia), there was more than a 60 per cent increase in the number of people suffering from asthma. In 1997, 40,000 Indonesians had to seek medical help for haze-related illnesses. The haze also killed six people in Indonesia.

Who did it?

In 2002, the Indonesian government banned the burning of forest land. However, fires in the forest continue to break out. Authorities suspect that plantation owners are still using fire to clear forest areas for their crops. The plantation owners claim that it is the weather that dries and heats the forest vegetation to **kindling point**. However, scientists say this is unlikely, as tropical forests are so moist they seldom reach kindling point in the heat of the Sun alone.

International fight against CFCs

In the 1980s, scientists discovered that the Earth's ozone layer was thinning. They realized that the main cause was the large amount of chlorofluorocarbons (CFCs) in the atmosphere. CFCs are compounds of the chemicals carbon, hydrogen and chlorine. They are released by factories, cars, **aerosol** cans and old refrigerators. CFCs remain in the atmosphere for as long as 40 years after they are released. This means that even if we stopped using CFCs today, the amount we have already released could harm the environment for the next 40 years.

Hole over Antarctica

In 1985, scientists from the British Antarctic Survey group realized that the atmosphere above Antarctica had lower-than-normal levels of ozone. The scientists warned that the thinning ozone allowed harmful ultraviolet (UV) rays to reach the Earth. Exposure to UV-B rays has been linked to an increased incidence of skin cancer and eye cataracts in humans.

The British Antarctic Survey's research station at Bird Island, South Georgia, Antarctica.

Rules and regulations

During the Vienna Convention in 1985, scientists and governments agreed to follow rules to protect the ozone in an international treaty. At that time, people still did not think that the thinning ozone was a big problem. Only 28 countries signed the treaty. In 1987, the United Nations Environmental Programme (UNEP) developed the Montreal Protocol on Substances that Deplete the Ozone Layer. The Montreal Protocol describes a set of rules and regulations limiting the use of substances, such as CFCs, that destroy the ozone layer.

Award-winning paintings by students for International Day for the Preservation of the Ozone Layer, held in Bangalore (India) on 16 September 2002. The aim was to spread awareness of ozone layer depletion in India. According to UNEP, India is responsible for releasing 16 per cent of the world production of CFCs into the environment.

Reducing CFCs

Under the Montreal Protocol, developing nations agreed to halve their CFC emissions and use by 2005. By 2007, UNEP hopes that the production and use of CFCs will have fallen by 85 per cent. In 2002, scientists found that the amount of ozone-destroying substances in the troposphere had already decreased. This was a direct result of the Montreal Protocol.

What happens to CFCs in the stratosphere?
In the stratosphere, UV rays break down CFCs to form atoms of chlorine (Cl). Each chlorine atom reacts with one atom of oxygen in ozone (O_3) to form chlorine monoxide (ClO) and oxygen gas (O_2). This reaction breaks down ozone. Chlorine monoxide (ClO) reacts with oxygen atoms (O) in the atmosphere, producing chlorine (Cl) and oxygen (O_2). The chlorine atom is then free to combine with more ozone molecules. So one molecule of a CFC can destroy hundreds and thousands of ozone molecules.

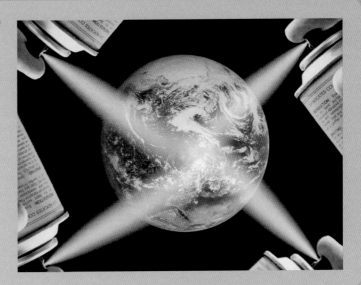

Green community

In 1994, health and environmental authorities found that 42 people in every 100,000 in Idaho (USA) die of air pollution-related respiratory diseases. Most of the air pollution came from Boise, Idaho's capital city. Boise lies in the south-west part of Idaho, along Boise River. Farmland spans Canyon County in the west and Ada in the south. Farmers frequently burn farmland to remove weeds and grow crops such as alfalfa. The burning releases particulate matter and adds to the air pollution. Through education, environmentally friendly programs and other means, Idaho's government, industries and residents are working together to fight air pollution in their state.

GEMStars

Idaho governor Dirk Kempthorne developed the GEMStars Program in 1999. The program educates members of the public on ways to prevent pollution from contaminating the environment. The program examines the practices of businesses, schools, governmental agencies and agricultural companies. Companies that show extraordinary commitment to protecting the environment receive public recognition.

Farmer tilling the land in Canyon County, Idaho.

Recycling wood stoves

Wood fires release large amounts of particulates. If particulates are inhaled, they irritate the lungs. The particulates and gases in wood smoke also contain cancer-causing substances. Residents in Idaho have been asked to trade in their old wood stoves for stoves that release less air pollution, such as pellet or gas stoves. To encourage the residents to use environmentally friendly stoves, the state government reduces taxes for people who trade their wood stoves in.

A traditional US wood stove.

Hybrid cars

Idaho car manufacturers are developing and selling hybrid vehicles. These are cars that run on a combination of conventional petroleum-powered engines and new electric motors. The hybrid cars use electricity when travelling at low speeds and when they need a boost to accelerate. These cars emit lower amounts of air pollution compared to ordinary vehicles. Hybrid vehicles release 10 per cent less smog-forming pollutants and 50 per cent less carbon dioxide.

This hybrid car is the first mass produced petroleum-electric hybrid vehicle introduced to North America.

Idaho National Guard

In August 2001, the Idaho National Guard (Air and Army) received the Idaho GEMStars award for environmental protection. Instead of travelling to work in individual cars, employees of the National Guard take turns to drive their colleagues to work. This reduces the number of cars on the road and therefore reduces air pollution. At the workplace, members of the National Guard travel around on bicycles or golf carts to get to and from various areas. These forms of transport do not cause air pollution.

The right to breathe fresh air

The Philippines is one of the most polluted places in Southeast Asia. Its capital, Manila, is one of the ten worst-polluted Asian cities. Smoke from the industries in Manila is so thick that residents have to walk around with handkerchiefs over their noses. Because of the air pollution, children as young as two months old are developing asthma.

Air pollution in Manila is not only caused by smoke from industries. Residents also have to put up with the stench from piles of uncollected rubbish on the city's sidewalks.

Reporting vehicles that emit exhaust fumes through text messaging is a positive way Filipinos can help clean up their environment.

Fighting air pollution with text messages

People living in the Philippines send up to 25 million text messages with their mobile phones every day. In 2002, Environmental Watchdog, a non-governmental organization (NGO) working in the country, started an anti-pollution campaign using text messaging.

Environmental Watchdog encourages anyone with a mobile phone to report vehicles emitting black exhaust fumes. They can do this by messaging the vehicle's licence plate number to the Land Transportation Office (LTO). The LTO contacts the vehicle owners and puts their vehicles through an exhaust test. Owners of vehicles that release high amounts of pollution have to get their engines checked and cleaned. Otherwise, these owners will lose their driving licences.

We want fresh air!

In 1999, the Filipino government passed a law banning the public burning of waste. Incineration industries and some politicians argued that the government should lift the ban. They said that burning waste is a good way of cleaning up the rubbish along the polluted city streets. They also proposed installing high-technology incinerators that would release minimal pollution.

People in power

NGOs including the Bantay Kalikasan collected millions of signatures from Filipinos in support of the ban. Lobby groups argued that air pollution, even in minimal amounts, is harmful to the environment and human health. They also said that high-technology incinerators would cost too much to maintain. The Filipino government kept the ban as a result of the overwhelming public concern.

Even children in the Philippines are doing their part to promote clean air. Here, they are participating at a rally organized by environmental activists.

Driving to their graves

Up to 33 per cent of **jeepney** drivers suffer from illnesses related to air pollution. These victims have breathing difficulties and excess phlegm in their throats. They are more vulnerable to tuberculosis and bronchitis. In 2003, it was estimated that more than 22 million Filipinos suffer from tuberculosis.

Global citizens

Air pollution damages all aspects of life. It is a global phenomenon. Air pollution causes thinning in the ozone layer, putting people at greater risk of developing skin cancer. Air pollution can be carried by winds from one country to another. Governments, multinational companies and multinational organizations like the World Health Organization (WHO) and the World Bank are working together towards cleaner air.

The Geneva Convention of Long-Range Transboundary Air Pollution

In the 1970s, scientists demonstrated that air pollution from one area could travel thousands of kilometres before the pollutants were deposited. This meant that international cooperation was necessary if countries wanted to keep their air clean. In 1979, the Geneva Convention of Long-Range **Transboundary** Air Pollution established guidelines for reducing the level of pollutants like sulphur emissions, nitrogen oxides and volatile organic compounds (VOCs). As of 5 August 2003, the European Community (EC) and 49 countries are listed as participants of the convention.

Nations unite

Governments of developing nations face the challenge of improving their economy through industrialization while keeping their air clean. Multinational organizations like the World Bank loan money to developing nations for environmentally friendly projects. For example, the World Bank has loaned US$570 million to help China build the Xiaolangdi hydroelectric dam in Henan Province. Each year, the Xiaolangdi Dam can generate 5.1 billion **kilowatt-hours** (kWh) of **hydroelectricity**, a pollution-free form of power. This amount of energy can power 1.5 million homes.

Construction of the Xiaolangdi Dam in Henan Province. Flowing through the province is the Huanghe or Yellow River, one of two great rivers in China.

Rice straw being harvested in the Philippines.

Foreign aid

Some multinational companies are helping to fight air pollution. In the Philippines, farmers traditionally burn rice straw after each harvest season, releasing air pollution and particulates into the environment. The Australian company Ortech Industries has developed a way to convert waste rice straw into wall panels for schools, houses and office buildings. Ortech engineers use the straw to make boards 5 centimetres thick and then place them on steel frames to build walls. Recycling rice straw reduces the amount of air pollution in the Philippines.

In a nutshell

Air pollution:

- causes short-term irritation like coughs and breathing difficulties to our respiratory systems
- causes more serious illnesses like cancer and heart disease if we live in polluted areas for long periods of time
- depletes the ozone layer
- contaminates soils.

Acid rain:

- destroys bridges and buildings, making our cities dangerous to live in
- corrodes statues, many of which are part of our historical heritage
- kills forests
- lowers the pH level of lakes and kills animals that cannot live in acidic environments.

What can I do?

Help conserve our environment! We can all do our part to protect the atmosphere from further pollution and clean up the local air. Here are some ways you can help.

Stationery made from recycled elephant dung paper, Colombo, Sri Lanka.

Recycle your rubbish

- Recycling reduces the amount of waste that is incinerated or buried in landfill sites.
- Use separate bins to sort your household rubbish into plastic, glass and paper products.
- Ask your parents or teacher where the nearest recycling site is and arrange a weekly visit to put each type of rubbish in the right bin.
- Find out if your local council has a scheme for collecting recyclable waste. The Green Box scheme in the UK is an example of such a program. Ask if you can participate in such a scheme.
- Set up a class project to reuse or recycle paper, cardboard and aluminium drink cans.
- Arrange a trip to a local recycling centre to see how rubbish can be turned into new products.

Campaign against air pollution

- Ask your teacher to help you find out about sources of air pollution in your area. You could ask local industries about their efforts to reduce pollution or look on the Internet pages of organizations like Greenpeace and Friends of the Earth.
- Write a class letter to your local MP or council telling them why you are worried about the sources of air pollution in your area. Ask questions about what the local authorities are doing to help keep your area clean.
- Ask your teacher to invite a local MP or council representative to talk to your class about pollution in your area.
- Use the information you collect to design a class poster telling the rest of the school about the risks of air pollution and what they can do to help fight it.

Going places

- Instead of taking the bus to a nearby destination, try cycling or walking there.
- Car pools are a great way to reduce the number of vehicles on the roads. If your parents are driving and picking you up from school, ask them to pick up other students living near you. That way, your friends' parents do not need to drive their cars to and from your school.
- Your parents and your friends' parents can take turns to take you and your friends to school.
- Organize a Walk to School day when everyone has to walk or cycle to school instead of travel by car. Make sure that you walk in a large group or with an adult to stay safe.

Protect yourself

- Ask your parents not to burn household rubbish in the garden; burning plastic, glue, batteries or rubber releases toxic fumes.
- Stay indoors when the air looks smoky outside.
- Wear a mask to cover your mouth and nose when you are working with things that may contain volatile organic compounds (VOCs), such as paint.
- Shake your blankets, pillows and stuffed toys outdoors regularly; this will help get rid of dust mites and dander.

London mayor Ken Livingstone on a bicycle to promote European Car Free Day, 13 September 2000.

Glossary

acid rain rain containing dissolved sulphur dioxide and nitrogen oxides

acidic substance with a sour taste and a pH level lower than seven. Strong acids can dissolve even metal.

aerosol cloud of fine solid or liquid particles suspended in a gas

alkaline having a pH level greater than seven. Alkaline substances often have a soapy feel and a bitter taste.

altitude height above sea level

amphibian cold-blooded, smooth-skinned animal that can live on land and in water. Frogs and salamanders are examples of amphibians.

atom smallest particle of a substance

bacteria microscopic organisms that have one cell and can cause disease

chlorophyll green pigment needed by plants to make food

component part that combines with other parts to make up a whole

corrosive having the ability to wear down or dissolve things

crustacean animal living in water and having a protective shell and limbs with joints. Examples of crustaceans include crabs, shrimps and lobsters.

cuticle waxy, protective layer that covers all parts of a plant

decomposition process in which organic matter is broken down

dissolve separate into molecules in a liquid

drought long period when there is no rain

emission substance discharged into the air

exhaust fumes released from a vehicle engine and other machine parts

fossil fuel fuel derived from the fossilized remains of plants and animals. Examples of fossil fuels are coal and petroleum.

frost injury damage to plants caused by the freezing of water inside them

gravitational force pull on objects by large objects like planets

heavy metal metallic substance that is harmful to our health. Heavy metals include lead, copper and mercury.

hemisphere one of the halves of the Earth on either side of the equator

humid hot and wet

hydroelectricity power that is generated from the force of rushing water

indicator something that changes colour in different environmental conditions. Scientists use the change to help them study environmental damage.

Industrial Revolution period between the 1700s and the 1800s when power-driven machinery began to replace human-powered tools

jeepney bus used as public transport in the Philippines

kilowatt-hour (kWh) a unit of electric power equal to the work done by one kilowatt, or 1000 watts, in one hour

kindling point temperature at which something catches fire

lichen fungus that grows on rocks, leaves or tree trunks. Lichens obtain their nourishment from the air and spread by producing spores.

malnutrition lack of proper nutrients like protein or vitamins

mould type of fungus. Many moulds can cause food to spoil.

mutate change in genetic make-up

neutral neither acidic nor alkaline. Neutral substances do not cause indicators to change colour.

nucleus core about which other parts are grouped or gathered

ozone gas that consists of three atoms of oxygen. Ozone protects us from ultraviolet (UV) rays in sunlight. In the troposphere, ozone is a component of smog.

particulate solid piece of material or liquid droplet in the air. Particulates may be so small that the human eye cannot see them.

percolate drain or seep through

photosynthesize make food in the presence of sunlight, carbon dioxide, chlorophyll and water. Only green plants photosynthesize.

pollutant substance that contaminates

pungent sharp and strong

quadruple increase by four times

radioactive decay spontaneous breakdown of material capable of releasing waves of energy

respire use oxygen to burn food to release energy

spore microorganism that helps fungi reproduce

stomata tiny holes in leaves that allow gas and water to pass

transboundary able to cross borders

ultraviolet (UV) invisible light rays in sunlight that can destroy skin cells and cause skin cancer

vaporize become gas

volatile organic compound (VOC) carbon-rich chemical that evaporates at room temperature

waste unwanted material

Finding out more

Books:

World's Worst Fire Disasters, Rob Alcraft
(Heinemann Library, 1999)

World's Worst Chemical Disasters, Rob Alcraft
(Heinemann Library, 1999)

World's Worst Nuclear Disasters, Rob Alcraft
(Heinemann Library, 1999)

Taking Action: Friends of the Earth, Louise Spilsbury
(Heinemann Library, 2000)

Taking Action: World Wide Fund for Nature, Louise
Spilsbury (Heinemann Library, 2000)

Just the Facts: Global Population, Paul Brown
(Heinemann Library, 2002)

Videos:

Acid Rain, American Lung Association (1984)

Industrial Ecology: The End of Industrialism,
EcoIntelligence Reports (2003)

Journey to Clear the Air, American Lung Association
(1992)

Subdivide and Conquer: A Modern Western, Bullfrog
Films (2003)

Urban Air: What's in the Sky, Blue Sky Associates
(2003)

What's in Our Air?, Rainbow and Film Productions
(1999)

Websites:

Encyclopedia of the Atmospheric Environment
http://www.doc.mmu.ac.uk/aric/eae/

Physicians for Social Responsibility
http://www.psr.org/breathe.htm

United Nations
http://earthwatch.unep.net/health/airpollution.php

UK National Air Quality Information Archive
http://www.airquality.co.uk/archive/index.php

Organizations:

Environmental Protection Agency (EPA)
Headquarters
Ariel Rios Building
1200 Pennsylvania Avenue, N.W.
Washington, DC 20460, USA
http://www.epa.gov/air/oaqps/index.html

Environmental Protection Agency (EPA)
40 City Road
Southbank, Victoria 3006, Australia
Phone: 03 9695 2722 Fax: 03 9695 2785
http://www.epa.vic.gov.au

Sierra Club
Headquarters
85 Second Street, 2nd Floor
San Francisco, CA 94105, USA
Phone: 415 977 5500 Fax: 415 977 5799
http://www.sierraclub.org

The American Lung Association
61 Broadway, 6th Floor
NY 10006, USA
Phone: 212 315 8700
http://www.lungusa.org/

National Society for Clean Air and Environmental
Protection (NSCA)
44, Grand Parade
Brighton BN2 9QA, UK
Phone: 01273 878770 Fax: 01273 606626
http://www.nsca.org.uk

Index